TERRIFIC TEAMS

Meet the KANSAS CITY CHIEFS

PERCY LEED

Lerner Publications ◆ Minneapolis

Stats in this book are accurate through the 2025 Super Bowl.

Lerner Publications Company
An imprint of Lerner Publishing Group, Inc.
241 First Avenue North
Minneapolis, MN 55401 USA

For reading levels and more information, look up this title at www.lernerbooks.com.

Main body text set in ITC Avant Garde Gothic Std.
Typeface provided by Adobe Systems.

Designer: Mary Ross **Photo Editor:** Cynthia Zemlicka
Lerner team: Sue Marquis

Library of Congress Cataloging-in-Publication Data

Names: Leed, Percy, 1968- author.
Title: Meet the Kansas City Chiefs / Percy Leed.
Description: Minneapolis, MN : Lerner Publications, [2026] | Series: Terrific teams (Lerner sports rookie) | Includes bibliographical references and index. | Audience: Ages 5–8 | Audience: Grades 2–3 | Summary: "With Patrick Mahomes and Travis Kelce leading the way, the Kansas City Chiefs have been the best team in the NFL since 2020. Explore the team's history, great moments, and modern superstars"— Provided by publisher.
Identifiers: LCCN 2024045570 (print) | LCCN 2024045571 (ebook) | ISBN 9798765668443 (library binding) | ISBN 9798765683675 (paperback) | ISBN 9798765681817 (epub)
Subjects: LCSH: Kansas City Chiefs (Football team)—Juvenile literature. | Football players—United States—Juvenile literature.
Classification: LCC GV956.K35 L44 2026 (print) | LCC GV956.K35 (ebook) | DDC 796.332/6409778411—dc23/eng/20241016

LC ebook record available at https://lccn.loc.gov/2024045571

Manufactured in the United States of America
1-1011739-53812-3/12/2025

Photo Acknowledgments
Jason Hanna/Getty Images, p. 5; Focus on Sport/Getty Images, p. 7; Roy Inman/Kansas City Star/Tribune News Service via Getty Images, p. 9; Erick W. Rasco/Sports Illustrated via Getty Images, p. 11; Peter Read Miller/Sports Illustrated via Getty Images, p. 13; Brian Bahr/Getty Images, p. 14; TIMOTHY A. CLARY/AFP via Getty Image, p. 17; Kevin C. Cox/Getty Images, p. 19; Nick Tre. Smith/Icon Sportswire via Getty Images, p. 20; Ezra Shaw/Getty Images, p. 22; David Eulitt/Getty Images, p. 23. Design elements: Kwangmoozaa/Getty Images; Andrii Shelenkov/Getty Images; AnthiaCumming/Getty Images.
Cover: Steve Sanders/Kansas City Chiefs via AP.

Table of Contents

★ CHAPTER 1 ★

Becoming the Chiefs

Patrick Mahomes ran with the football. He threw a pass to Travis Kelce.

Kelce caught the ball. He scored a touchdown for the Kansas City Chiefs!

The Chiefs used to be the Dallas Texans.

In 1963, the Texans moved to Kansas City, Missouri. They changed their name to the Chiefs.

★ CHAPTER 2 ★

Big Moments

In 1967, the Chiefs played in the first Super Bowl. They lost to the Green Bay Packers.

Three years later, the Chiefs won their first Super Bowl. They beat the Minnesota Vikings 23–7.

After beating the Vikings, the Chiefs didn't play in the Super Bowl again for 50 years.

From 2020 to 2024, the Chiefs won the Super Bowl three times.

★ CHAPTER 3 ★

Best Players

Quarterback Len Dawson played 13 seasons with the Chiefs. He helped the team win 93 games.

Derrick Thomas was a tough defender. He had 20 sacks in 1990.

Running back Priest Holmes was a great scorer. He scored 83 total touchdowns in 65 Chiefs games.

Many fans say Chiefs tight end Tony Gonzalez was the best tight end ever. He was good at catching passes.

Travis Kelce is another great Chiefs tight end. He has won three Super Bowls with the team.

Quarterback Patrick Mahomes is an NFL superstar. He has been the Super Bowl MVP three times.

★ CHAPTER 4 ★

Super Team

The Chiefs have won four Super Bowls. Only four teams have won more.

Andy Reid has coached the team since 2013. He has never had a losing season with the Chiefs.

allegiant stadium
SUPER BOWL LVIII
SUPER BOWL CHAMPIONS
CHIEFS

The Chiefs won the Super Bowl in 2020, 2023, and 2024. They reached the big game again in 2025. But they lost to the Philadelphia Eagles.

Can Mahomes lead the Chiefs to another Super Bowl? Fans can't wait to see!

KANSAS CITY CHIEFS TEAM LEADERS

Passing touchdowns:	Patrick Mahomes, 245
Passing yards:	Patrick Mahomes, 32,352
Rushing yards:	Jamaal Charles, 7,260
Rushing touchdowns:	Priest Holmes, 76
Tackles:	Derrick Johnson, 941

Glossary

MVP: most valuable player

NFL: National Football League

sack: when a quarterback is tackled for a loss of yards

Learn More

Downs, Kieran. *Football*. Minneapolis: Bellwether Media, 2024.

Huddleston, Emma. *Get Ready for a Football Game*. Minneapolis: Bearport, 2024.

Leed, Percy. *Football's Super Bowl*. Minneapolis: Lerner Publications, 2025.

Index